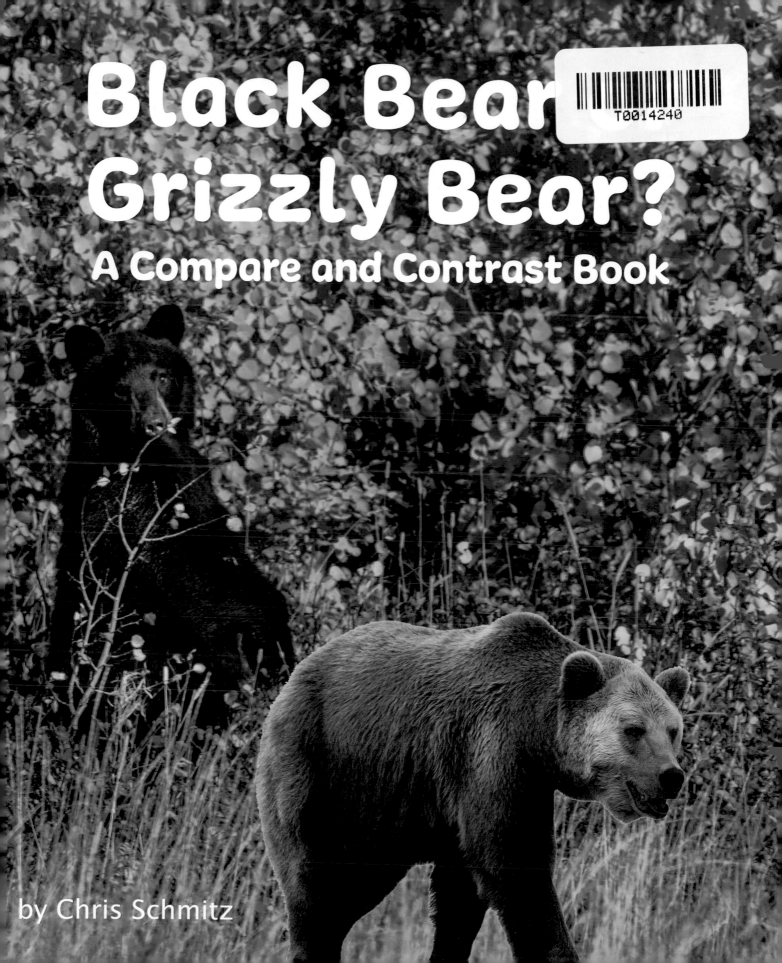

Black Bear Grizzly Bear?

A Compare and Contrast Book

by Chris Schmitz

Bears are mammals that belong to the family Ursidae. There are eight different species, or kinds, of bears that live on earth today: the Asiatic black bear, brown bear, giant panda, North American black bear, polar bear, sloth bear, spectacled bear, and sun bear.

Asiatic black bear

brown bear

giant panda

North American black bear

They all have big bodies with short legs, rounded ears, thick fur, and tiny tails. They walk on the soles of their entire feet. Bears have five claws on each paw that cannot be pulled in like a cat's.

In North America, there are three species of bears: the brown bear, the black bear, and the polar bear.

polar bear

sloth bear

spectacled bear

sun bear

Black bears in North America are divided into 16 subspecies based on minor differences in their looks and DNA. Some of their common names include Eastern black bears, Kermode bears, cinnamon bears, and glacier bears, but they are all black bears.

Black bears live in a variety of habitats throughout North America. These include forests, swamps, and mountain meadows.

Eastern black bear

Kermode bear

Cinnamon bear

Brown bears in North America are divided into three groups based on how they look and where they live: Kodiak brown bears, grizzly bears, and coastal brown bears.

Grizzly bears are found in the inland parts of North America. They usually live in thick forests, high mountain meadows, and mountain valleys.

Kodiak

Grizzly bear

Coastal brown bear

Just like humans have different-colored hair, so do bears—even brothers and sisters!

Despite being named black bears for their fur color, not all black bears are black. They can be brown, cinnamon, blond, or a combination of light and dark hair. A group of black bears in British Columbia, Canada, called the Kermode or spirit bears, are white.

brown black bear mom with black and cinnamon cubs

Kermode mom with black cub

multi-colors

Grizzly bears get their name from the silvery, blond-tipped hairs on their back and shoulders. Not all grizzlies are "grizzled," but they do come in a lot of colors. They can be pale blond to reddish-blond, light brown, darker brown, or almost black.

grizzled

blond

black

brown

From the side, black bears have a straight line from forehead to nose tip and look more like a dog.

Their muzzles are often a light-brown color.

Black bears have large ears that are long, upright, and pointed. They also have a flatter, shorter fur coat than a grizzly.

Black bears have short, dark, and sharply-curved claws. Their claws are one to two inches long. They use them for ripping into rotten logs, looking for bugs, shallow digging, making dens, and climbing trees.

From the side, grizzly bears have dish-shaped heads. There is a curve running between their eyes to the end of their noses.

Their muzzles are wide and easy to see. Their eyes look very close together.

Grizzly bears have small, rounded ears compared to their head size. Their fur is longer and fluffier than a black bear's.

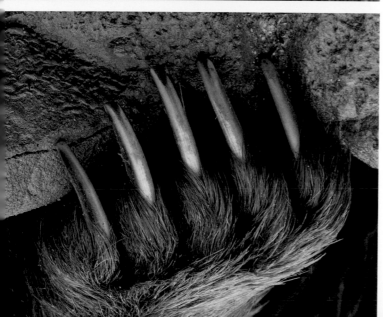

Adult grizzly bears have gently-curved claws. Their claws can be two to four inches long. They use their nails for digging roots, dens, and uncovering small prey like grubs and pika.

Black bears do not have a shoulder hump.

When standing on all fours, their rump is higher than the rest of the body.

Grizzly bears have well-developed shoulder muscles for digging and turning over rocks. These muscles look like a big hump between their front shoulders.

When standing on all four feet, a grizzly's rump is lower than its hump.

Bears have good eyesight and can see in color. Their sense of smell is excellent. Researchers tracked a black bear for three miles, following the scent of a dead deer. They use their sense of smell to find food and mates, detect dangers, and navigate.

Both black and grizzly bears will stand on their hind legs to see and smell their surroundings.

Both black bears and grizzly bears are omnivores—meaning they eat both plants and meat. They eat a lot of food in the late summer and fall. Storing fat helps them to get through the cold winter months.

Black bears will eat just about anything they find. They eat grasses, roots, berries, insects, fish, and mammals.

Black bears' diets are 90 percent plants and 10 percent protein (meat).

10%

90%

Like black bears, grizzly bears also eat grasses, berries, roots, bugs, and fish. They will also prey upon young deer, elk, and bison. They also scavenge from wolf kills.

Grizzly bears' diets are about 75 percent plants and 25 percent protein (meat).

25%

75%

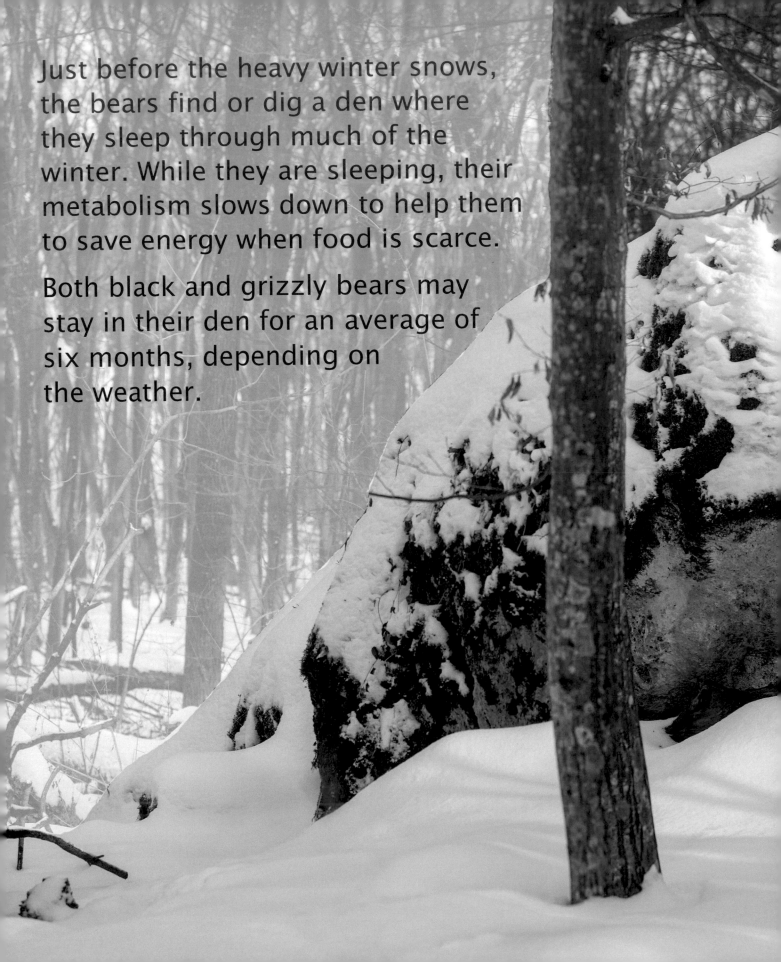

Just before the heavy winter snows, the bears find or dig a den where they sleep through much of the winter. While they are sleeping, their metabolism slows down to help them to save energy when food is scarce.

Both black and grizzly bears may stay in their den for an average of six months, depending on the weather.

If a female bear, or sow, is pregnant, she gives birth in her den to her cubs. The male bears, called boars, are in separate burrows, sleeping and waiting for warmer weather and the plants to grow.

Both black and grizzly bears have between 2 and 4 cubs at a time. The tiny cubs are about eight inches long and weigh less than a pound at birth, about the same size and weight as a can of soda. The cubs are helpless at birth and cannot see, hear, smell, walk, and have no teeth.

The cubs grow rapidly by drinking their mother's fat-rich milk. By spring, they are ready to leave the den and play and climb. The sows continue to feed their babies milk. As they get bigger, she teaches them how to find other foods and stay safe.

Black bear cubs stay with their mothers for at least one year after their births. Grizzly bear cubs stay with their mothers for about three years before heading out on their own.

Bears play an essential role in the environment. As omnivores, they eat both other animals and plants.

As predators, they help keep the numbers of rodents, deer, and elk in balance. And they clean up carcasses left by other predators.

Their eating of plants and berries helps spread seeds every time they leave a fertilizing pile of scat behind.